MOBILE APP DEVELOPMENT 101: CREATING FOR ANDROID AND IOS

Table of Contents

- Introduction
  - The Evolution of Mobile Apps
  - Importance of Mobile App Literacy
  - Native vs. Hybrid vs. Web Apps

Chapter 1: Understanding Mobile Platforms

- Overview of Android and iOS Ecosystems
- Market Share and User Demographics
- Hardware and Software Differences

Chapter 2: Setting up the Development Environment

- Android: Android Studio and SDK
- iOS: Xcode and iOS SDK
- Emulators and Real Device Testing

Chapter 3: Basics of Android Development

- Understanding Android App Architecture
- Activities, Intents, and Fragments
- Designing UI with XML
- Handling User Interactions

Chapter 4: Dive into iOS Development

- Fundamentals of iOS App Architecture
- View Controllers and Storyboards
- Swift Language Basics
- Designing Interfaces with UIKit

Chapter 5: Cross-Platform Mobile App Tools

- Introduction to Flutter, React Native, and Xamarin
- Pros and Cons of Cross-Platform Development
- Building a Simple App on a Cross-Platform Tool

Chapter 6: Design Principles for Mobile Apps

- Importance of User Experience (UX) and User Interface

INTRODUCTION

In an increasingly connected world, mobile devices have become an indispensable part of our daily lives. From morning alarms to late-night social media browsing, checking the weather to video calling across continents, mobile apps influence almost every facet of modern life. These powerful pocket computers —smartphones—house a universe of possibilities, all unlocked through the magic of mobile applications. If you've picked up this book, you're likely intrigued by this magic and wish to become a creator in the realm of mobile app development. Welcome to "Mobile App Development 101: Creating for Android and iOS."

This book is tailored for enthusiasts taking their first step into the world of mobile app development. Whether you come from a background in web development, are a seasoned programmer in other languages, or are an absolute beginner, the subsequent chapters promise a journey tailored to demystify the complexities of creating apps for the world's two dominant mobile platforms: Android and iOS.

While Android and iOS cater to vast user bases, each has its unique ecosystem, development environment, and user expectations.

This book aims to provide a balanced insight into both worlds, allowing you to appreciate their individual strengths and challenges. As we delve into the intricacies of each platform, you'll gain hands-on experience, build foundational skills, and foster an understanding of the philosophies that underpin Android and iOS development.

Yet, the world of mobile app development isn't limited to these two giants. With the rise of cross-platform tools, developers now wield the power to write code once and deploy on multiple platforms. We'll touch upon this revolution, giving you a glimpse of tools like Flutter, React Native, and Xamarin, and the opportunities they present.

As you progress through the chapters, remember that while tools and technologies evolve, the principles of creating intuitive, user-friendly, and impactful apps remain constant. Embrace challenges, seek feedback, and iterate. After all, every app, from the simplest utility to the most groundbreaking innovation, starts with a single line of code.

So, whether you aspire to bring a unique app idea to life, enhance your existing development skills, or simply quench your curiosity about mobile app creation, this book is your companion. Let's embark on this exciting journey together, transforming from app users to app creators.

Happy coding!

CHAPTER 1: UNDERSTANDING MOBILE PLATFORMS

The world of mobile devices is diverse and ever-evolving, with two mainstays at its core: Android and iOS. Together, they encapsulate the lion's share of the global mobile operating system market, solidifying their place as the primary platforms for mobile developers.

Overview of Android and iOS Ecosystems

Android, helmed by Google, takes pride in its open-source nature, paving the way for its adoption by a myriad of device manufacturers. This results in an expansive device ecosystem that spans budget-friendly smartphones to luxury flagship devices. Android's versatility has also spawned various custom versions (or "skins") of the operating system, each with its set of features built upon the foundational Android platform.

iOS, Apple's brainchild, operates within a more controlled realm. Exclusive to Apple devices like iPhones, iPads, and iPod Touches, iOS offers a consistent user experience, punctuated by regular software updates and a carefully curated App Store. While the ecosystem is more restricted, developers benefit from uniformity, albeit with strict guidelines.

Market Share and User Demographics

In terms of sheer numbers, Android's global market share is formidable, thanks to its diverse array of devices and price points. However, iOS carves out its niche, especially in markets with higher purchasing power. Recognizing these nuances can be invaluable, helping developers tailor their applications to resonate with specific audiences. For instance, Android's dominance in emerging markets contrasts with iOS's strong foothold in regions with higher disposable incomes.

Hardware and Software Differences

On the hardware front, Android's vastness is evident. Its open architecture means it integrates with a range of device specifications, from varying screen sizes to diverse processors. This presents a dual-edged sword for developers: a broad user base on one hand and the challenge of ensuring device compatibility on the other.

In contrast, iOS offers more hardware consistency due to its limited device range. However, developers must still cater to the varied specifications of different iPhone and iPad models.

When it comes to software, Android's fragmentation is both a challenge and an opportunity. Multiple Android versions across devices mean developers need to ensure broad compatibility. However, the platform's open nature offers unparalleled integration flexibility. Conversely, iOS's consistent and swift updates often mean that users migrate to the latest version quickly. This allows developers to tap into new features, but they must also remain agile, adapting to Apple's frequent software evolutions.

CHAPTER 2: SETTING UP THE DEVELOPMENT ENVIRONMENT

Before diving into the intricacies of mobile app development, it's essential to ensure that your development environment is appropriately set up. This chapter will guide you through the necessary tools and configurations for both Android and iOS, offering a seamless beginning to your development journey.

Android: Android Studio and SDK

Android Studio is the official integrated development environment (IDE) for Android app development. It offers a comprehensive suite of tools tailored for Android, from a powerful code editor to emulators for testing.

Setting Up Android Studio:

1. Download and Install: Head to the official Android Developer website to download the latest version of Android Studio.
2. Initial Setup: Launch Android Studio and follow the setup wizard, which will guide you through the installation of necessary components, including the Android Software Development Kit (SDK).
3. Configure the Android Emulator: Android Studio provides a built-in emulator to test apps. Ensure you configure one with desired device specifications to emulate real-world testing scenarios.

iOS: Xcode and iOS SDK

Xcode is Apple's official development environment for iOS. It is robust, integrating everything you need for iOS and macOS app development.

Setting Up Xcode:

1. Download and Install: Xcode is available on the Mac App Store. Ensure you have a Mac, as iOS development is exclusive to Apple's macOS.
2. Signing in with an Apple ID: Upon launching Xcode, sign in with your Apple ID. If you aim to deploy apps to the App Store, consider enrolling in the Apple Developer Program.
3. Simulators: Xcode offers simulators for various Apple devices, from iPhones to iPads. Familiarize yourself with these simulators to test your apps on different screen sizes and resolutions.

Emulators and Real Device Testing

While emulators and simulators provide an invaluable

environment for initial testing, it's crucial to also test apps on actual devices. This ensures compatibility and helps identify real-world issues that might not manifest in a simulated environment.

For Android:

1. Enable Developer Mode: On your Android device, navigate to 'Settings' > 'About phone' and tap the 'Build number' multiple times.
2. USB Debugging: In the now accessible 'Developer options', enable 'USB debugging'.
3. Connect to Android Studio: Using a USB cable, connect your device to your computer. Android Studio should recognize it, allowing for direct app installations and testing.

For iOS:

1. Register Your Device with Apple: Log in to the Apple Developer website and register your device's UDID (Unique Device Identifier).
2. Deployment from Xcode: With your iOS device connected to your Mac, you can select it as a build target in Xcode and deploy your app directly for testing.

Setting up a development environment might feel daunting at first, but with the right tools and configurations, it becomes a streamlined process. With your environment now ready, you're poised to start crafting mobile applications, bringing your ideas to life on Android and iOS platforms. The next chapter will introduce you to the world of Android development, diving deep into its architecture and nuances.

CHAPTER 3: BASICS OF ANDROID DEVELOPMENT

Android, being the most widely adopted mobile OS globally, offers a vast canvas for developers. Its open ecosystem and diverse device range present both opportunities and challenges. This chapter will demystify the foundational concepts of Android development, setting you on a path to create intuitive, scalable, and engaging applications for a plethora of Android devices.

Understanding Android App Architecture

Every Android app rests on a unique architecture, comprising components that define how the app functions and interacts with the system and users. Key components include:

1. Activities: Represent a single screen with a user

interface. Every app has one or more activities to guide user interactions.

2. Services: Perform background tasks without a user interface. These can run in the background, even if the user is not interacting with the app.

3. Broadcast Receivers: Respond to system-wide announcements or broadcasts. For example, an app can receive a notification when the device loses network connectivity.

4. Content Providers: Manage shared app data, allowing data storage and retrieval across different apps using a structured interface.

Activities, Intents, and Fragments

- Activities: The primary UI component of an Android app. Each screen the user interacts with is typically an activity. Activities have a lifecycle, transitioning through stages like "started," "paused," and "stopped."
- Intents: The messaging system used to request an action from another app component. For instance, using an intent, one activity can start another or send data between them.
- Fragments: Represent a behavior or part of the user interface within an Activity. They allow for more modular and flexible UI designs, especially on devices with larger screens like tablets.

Designing UI with XML

Android uses XML (eXtensible Markup Language) for designing and specifying app layouts. XML provides a structured, readable way to define UI elements like buttons, text views, and images.

For example:

```
<Button                         android:id="@+id/myButton"
android:layout_width="wrap_content"
android:layout_height="wrap_content" android:text="Click Me!" /
>
```

The XML code above defines a simple button with a label "Click Me!"

Handling User Interactions

User interactions are at the heart of any mobile application. In Android, listeners capture these events. For instance, when a user taps a button, an OnClickListener can be used to define the action that should be taken:

```
Button      myButton      =      findViewById(R.id.myButton);
myButton.setOnClickListener(new         View.OnClickListener()
{ @Override public void onClick(View v) { // Handle the button
click action here } });
```

Embarking on the Android development journey requires an understanding of its foundational elements, from app architecture to user interactions. With this knowledge, you're equipped to dive deeper into the world of Android, crafting applications that resonate with users and leverage the platform's capabilities to the fullest. The following chapters will expand on these concepts, exploring the richness of Android development further.

CHAPTER 4: DIVE INTO IOS DEVELOPMENT

While Android offers the broadest reach in terms of user base, iOS stands out for its uniformity, consistent user experience, and loyal customer base. Developing for iOS means entering Apple's ecosystem, with its specific tools, guidelines, and best practices. This chapter will immerse you in the world of iOS development, unraveling its core principles and techniques.

Fundamentals of iOS App Architecture

iOS apps boast a structured architecture, with several layers dictating their operation:

1. User Interface: This is where interactions happen, consisting of elements like buttons, tables, and navigation controls.
2. Application (or App Logic): The core engine of your

app, housing the custom code and managing user interactions.

3. Core Services: Providing essential services like networking, file access, and contact management.
4. Media: Handling audio, video, graphics, and other media-related functionalities.
5. Core OS: The base layer that interfaces directly with device hardware.

View Controllers and Storyboards

- View Controllers: These are the linchpins of your iOS application, managing individual screens or views. They dictate the content displayed on the screen and handle user interactions.
- Storyboards: A graphical representation of the UI, Storyboards allow developers to design app interfaces using a drag-and-drop interface in Xcode. They visually represent the app's flow and the relationships between individual view controllers.

Swift Language Basics

Swift, Apple's programming language, is integral to iOS development. It offers a combination of performance and modern syntax:

- Variables and Constants:
var myVariable = 10 let myConstant = 20

- Conditional Statements:

if myVariable < myConstant { print("Variable is less than constant.") } else { print("Variable is equal to or greater than constant.") }

- Loops:

for i in 1...5 { print("This is loop iteration \(i)") }

- Functions:

func greet(name: String) -> String { return "Hello, \(name)!" }

Designing Interfaces with UIKit

UIKit, the foundational framework for UI design in iOS, provides a plethora of elements, from buttons to sliders:

let button = UIButton(type: .system) button.frame = CGRect(x: 50, y: 50, width: 200, height: 40) button.setTitle("Click Me", for: .normal)

Navigating the iOS development landscape requires a nuanced understanding of its tools, languages, and design principles. With the foundation set, you're primed to delve deeper, harnessing the capabilities of iOS to craft applications that both dazzle and deliver. The journey continues with further exploration into iOS's vast offerings and a dive into cross-platform tools that bridge the Android-iOS divide.

CHAPTER 4: DIVE INTO IOS DEVELOPMENT

iOS stands out in the mobile world with its unique blend of uniformity, a consistent user experience, and a devoted customer base. As you delve into iOS development, you'll be immersing yourself in Apple's intricate ecosystem, characterized by specific tools, stringent guidelines, and best practices. Let's embark on this iOS journey, exploring its foundational principles and techniques.

Fundamentals of iOS App Architecture

At the heart of any iOS application lies a robust and structured architecture:

1. User Interface: The layer where all user interactions happen, containing elements such as buttons, tables, and navigation controls.
2. Application (or App Logic): This section houses your

custom code, which manages user interactions and drives the app's core functionalities.

3. Core Services: A layer that provides pivotal services like file access, networking, and contact management.
4. Media: This handles all media-related functionalities, such as audio, graphics, video, and animations.
5. Core OS: Positioned at the base, it directly interfaces with device hardware, ensuring optimal performance and stability.

View Controllers and Storyboards

- View Controllers: Central to any iOS application, view controllers manage and dictate the content of individual screens, handling the myriad user interactions.
- Storyboards: This visual tool allows developers to craft app interfaces using Xcode's intuitive drag-and-drop functionality. Storyboards vividly portray the app's flow, illustrating the connections between various view controllers.

Swift Language Basics

Swift is the beating heart of iOS development. Apple's proprietary language, Swift melds performance with a contemporary syntax:

- Variables and Constants:
var myVariable = 10 let myConstant = 20

- Conditional Statements:

```
if myVariable < myConstant { print("Variable is less than
constant.") } else { print("Variable is equal to or greater than
constant.") }
```

- Loops:

```
for i in 1...5 { print("This is loop iteration \(i)") }
```

- Functions:

```
func greet(name: String) -> String { return "Hello, \(name)!" }
```

Designing Interfaces with UIKit

UIKit stands as the cornerstone for UI design in iOS, equipping developers with an extensive array of interface elements:

```
let button = UIButton(type: .system) button.frame = CGRect(x:
50, y: 50, width: 200, height: 40) button.setTitle("Click Me",
for: .normal)
```

As you journey deeper into the realm of iOS, the framework you've built in this chapter will be instrumental. With a solid understanding of the tools, languages, and principles, you're set to further explore and leverage iOS's extensive capabilities. The subsequent chapters promise a deeper dive and more intricate explorations.

CHAPTER 5: CROSS-PLATFORM MOBILE APP TOOLS

In the evolving landscape of mobile app development, the dichotomy of Android and iOS development is met with a third paradigm: cross-platform development. Cross-platform tools promise the allure of "write once, run everywhere." This chapter will introduce you to the world of cross-platform mobile app development, exploring the prominent tools and their potential.

Introduction to Flutter, React Native, and Xamarin

- Flutter: Developed by Google, Flutter allows developers to create natively compiled applications for mobile, web, and desktop from a single codebase. It uses the Dart programming language and boasts a rich set of customizable widgets for creating complex UIs.
- React Native: Spearheaded by Facebook, React Native lets

you build mobile apps using only JavaScript. It provides a suite of native components, allowing you to retain the look, feel, and functionality of native apps.

- Xamarin: Backed by Microsoft, Xamarin uses C# for coding, allowing developers to share code across multiple platforms. With Xamarin, you can create native UIs and access platform-specific APIs.

Pros and Cons of Cross-Platform Development

- Advantages:
  - Code Reusability: A significant portion of the code can be used across platforms, speeding up development.
  - Cost-Effective: Managing one codebase can reduce developmental costs.
  - Uniform Look and Feel: Ensure consistent UI/UX across Android and iOS.
- Drawbacks:
  - Performance Concerns: While advancements are bridging the gap, native apps can sometimes outperform cross-platform ones.
  - Platform-Specific Limitations: Not all native features might be accessible or easy to implement.
  - Increased Complexity: Some customizations might require platform-specific code, negating the "write once" principle.

Building a Simple App on a Cross-Platform Tool

For a hands-on experience, let's explore a basic example using React Native

1. Setup: Begin by installing Node.js, then use npm to install the React Native CLI.

npm install -g react-native-cli

2. Creating a New App:

react-native init SimpleApp

3. Running the App: Navigate to your app's directory and initiate it.

cd SimpleApp react-native run-ios or react-native

4. Editing the App: Open App.js in a text editor and modify the default content. Saving the changes will instantly reflect in the running app, thanks to React Native's hot reload feature.

With the rise of cross-platform tools, the mobile app development field continues to democratize. Developers now have the flexibility to choose the best path according to the project's requirements, whether it's going native or harnessing the power of cross-platform solutions. As you explore further, you'll find that each approach, be it native or cross-platform, has its unique offerings, challenges, and rewards.

CHAPTER 6: DESIGN PRINCIPLES FOR MOBILE APPS

An app's success isn't solely determined by its functionality; the design plays a pivotal role. Good design isn't just about aesthetics; it's about ensuring an intuitive, user-friendly experience. This chapter delves into the principles that underpin effective mobile app design, providing you with insights to create applications that resonate with users.

Importance of User Experience (UX) and User Interface (UI)

- User Experience (UX): UX pertains to a user's overall experience when interacting with an app. It encompasses the app's functionality, usability, and the emotions evoked during use. A seamless UX ensures that users can easily achieve their goals within the app.
- User Interface (UI): UI is the series of screens, pages,

buttons, and visual elements that enable users to interact with an app. A compelling UI is visually appealing, easy to navigate, and aligned with modern design principles.

Mobile Design Patterns and Best Practices

1. Consistency: The app's design elements and actions should remain consistent across the platform. This consistency provides users with a predictable and comfortable experience.
2. Simplicity: A clean, uncluttered interface helps users focus on essential tasks. Overloading an app with features can confuse and deter users.
3. Feedback & Response: Whether it's a button press or a completed action, always provide feedback to users, letting them know the app is processing their request.
4. Intuitive Navigation: Navigational elements, such as menus or tabs, should be clear and easily accessible, allowing users to move seamlessly through the app.
5. Adaptive Design: With a multitude of device sizes and resolutions, ensure your app's design is responsive and adaptive to various screens.

Responsiveness, Gestures, and Animations

- Responsiveness: An app should respond swiftly to user interactions. Delays, even if minor, can frustrate users and lead to app abandonment.

- Gestures: Touch gestures like swiping, pinching, and tapping have become second nature to users. Incorporate common gestures in your app but ensure they're consistent with general expectations.
- Animations: While animations can enhance an app's appeal, overusing or poorly executing them can be detrimental. Use animations to guide, inform, or delight users, but always ensure they serve a purpose and are optimized for performance.

Effective mobile app design stems from a blend of aesthetics and functionality. By adhering to established design principles and continually seeking feedback, you can create apps that not only look great but also offer an exceptional user experience. As the digital landscape evolves, so do design methodologies, and staying attuned to these shifts will ensure your apps remain relevant, engaging, and user-centric.

CHAPTER 7: MOBILE APP TESTING AND DEBUGGING

Once an app is designed and developed, the process doesn't end. Thorough testing and debugging are vital to ensure that the app functions as intended and offers a seamless experience to the users. This chapter will guide you through the various facets of mobile app testing, equipping you with the knowledge to release robust, high-quality applications.

The Mobile App Testing Process

Every app should undergo rigorous testing before it's launched to the public. Here's a structured approach to mobile app testing:

1. Unit Testing: Testing individual units or components of the software in isolation. This helps in quickly identifying and rectifying issues at the code level.

2. Integration Testing: After unit testing, different components are combined and tested as a group, ensuring they work harmoniously.
3. System Testing: The entire system undergoes testing under this phase to ensure it meets the specified requirements.
4. Acceptance Testing: This determines whether the system complies with the user requirements and if it's ready for release.

Tools for Testing Mobile Apps

There are several tools available to assist with mobile app testing:

1. JUnit: Popular for unit testing in Android.
2. Espresso: For Android UI testing.
3. XCTest: Used for unit and UI testing in iOS.
4. Appium: An open-source tool suitable for cross-platform app testing.

Debugging Common Issues on Android and iOS

Debugging is the process of identifying and resolving issues (bugs) in your app. Both Android and iOS platforms provide robust tools to aid debugging:

- For Android:
  - Logcat: Available in Android Studio, Logcat captures system logs which can be invaluable in tracing issues.

- Android Profiler: This tool provides real-time data about your app's memory, CPU, and network activities.
- For iOS:
  - LLDB Debugger: Integrated into Xcode, LLDB helps in inspecting and controlling the app's execution.
  - Instruments: A performance analysis and testing tool that comes with Xcode, allowing developers to monitor and improve app performance.

Emulators vs. Real Device Testing

While emulators and simulators can replicate many functionalities of real devices, testing on actual devices is indispensable:

- Advantages of Real Device Testing:
  - Accurate performance metrics.
  - Real-world testing of features like camera, GPS, gestures, etc.
  - Better understanding of the look and feel on actual devices.
- Limitations of Emulators:
  - Might not replicate all hardware features.
  - Performance can differ from real devices.

Thorough testing and debugging are paramount to ensure

the delivery of a quality app. They help identify areas of improvement, ensuring that the final product offers an exceptional user experience without any glitches. As technology and user expectations evolve, continuous testing and iterative improvement become the cornerstones of successful app development. The subsequent chapters will explore the final stages of the app development journey, focusing on deployment and navigating the dynamic world of app stores.

CHAPTER 8: DEPLOYING AND DISTRIBUTING MOBILE APPS

After the arduous journey of designing, developing, and testing a mobile app, the next crucial phase is deployment and distribution. Ensuring that your app reaches your target audience efficiently requires an understanding of app stores, their guidelines, and the nuances of the deployment process. This chapter will guide you through the final steps of bringing your mobile app to the masses.

Understanding App Stores: Google Play and Apple App Store

- Google Play Store: This is the official app store for Android devices. With millions of apps and billions of downloads, it's a primary platform for Android developers to distribute their apps.

- Apple App Store: Exclusively for iOS apps, the App Store has a reputation for its stringent review processes and quality control. Although the number of apps is lower than the Play Store, the App Store often boasts higher revenue generation for developers.

Preparing for Deployment

Before deploying, a checklist ensures your app adheres to necessary guidelines:

1. Optimize Performance: Ensure your app runs smoothly, with quick load times and efficient memory usage.
2. Final Testing: Conduct a last round of testing, especially on the target devices and OS versions.
3. Set Up App Icons and Screenshots: Prepare high-quality app icons and screenshots as they play a pivotal role in app listings.
4. Determine Pricing: Decide whether your app will be free, paid, or include in-app purchases.
5. Review Store Guidelines: Both Google and Apple have specific guidelines. Familiarize yourself with these to ensure your app gets approved.

Deployment Process

- For Android:
    1. Create an APK: The APK (Android Package) is the package file format used by the Android OS

for distribution and installation of apps.
2. Sign Your App: A digitally signed APK ensures it's secure and comes from a known entity.
3. Set Up a Google Play Developer Account: There's a one-time fee for registration.
4. Upload Your App: Provide all required information, upload the APK, and submit it for review.

- For iOS:
  1. Code Signing: Apple requires apps to be signed with a developer identity to ensure it originates from a known source.
  2. Set Up an Apple Developer Account: There's an annual fee for the Apple Developer Program.
  3. Upload Using Xcode: Once ready, use Xcode to upload your app to the App Store.
  4. Submit for Review: Apple's review process is thorough, ensuring apps meet their quality and security standards.

Post-Deployment Strategies

1. Monitoring and Analytics: Use tools like Google Analytics or Flurry to monitor user engagement and app performance.
2. User Feedback: Encourage users to leave reviews and ratings, and be proactive in addressing their concerns or feedback.
3. Regular Updates: Keep your app updated with new features, bug fixes, and improvements to ensure it remains relevant and efficient.

CARTER

CONCLUSION: THE JOURNEY OF MOBILE APP MASTERY

Navigating the multifaceted world of mobile app development is akin to embarking on an epic journey. Starting from the foundational understanding of platforms and programming, to delving into design intricacies, testing paradigms, and scaling strategies, each phase presents its unique challenges and rewards.

Throughout this guide, we've journeyed together through the essential stages of app creation, from conceptualization to deployment and beyond. But remember, in the ever-evolving digital landscape, learning and adaptation never truly cease. The tools, techniques, and best practices will continually shift as technology advances and user preferences change.

As you move forward, armed with the knowledge amassed from this book, never lose sight of the core principle that underpins successful app development: value creation. Whether it's solving a pressing problem, entertaining users, or bridging a gap in the digital ecosystem, ensuring genuine value will always remain at the heart of any successful mobile application.

Continue to embrace feedback, stay curious, and remain adaptable. With every app you develop, you're not just coding software; you're crafting experiences, solving problems, and potentially touching millions of lives. Here's to your success, growth, and the countless innovations you'll bring to the world of mobile app development!

Thank you for allowing this guide to be a part of your journey. The world awaits your digital creations. Forge ahead, and happy coding!